THE ENCOURAGEMENT SERIES

I0459330

JOY

ONE-MONTH DEVOTIONAL

RUTH HOVSEPIAN

JOY: A One-Month Devotional

Copyright © 2025 by Ruth Hovsepian

Interior & cover design by Ruth Hovsepian

Paperback ISBN: 978-1-962581-78-3
eBook ISBN: 978-1-962581-79-0

To everyone searching for joy
in the middle of life's storms—
This book is for you.

Dear Friend,

Life is full of seasons—some bright with laughter, others heavy with burdens. My prayer is that this book will meet you wherever you are and remind you that joy is possible, not because life is easy, but because God is faithful.

Each day in this devotional has been designed with simplicity and encouragement in mind:

- **A Key Verse** to focus your heart and mind on God's promises.
- **A Thought that** expands on the verse and offers practical encouragement for daily living.
- **A Prayer** to guide you in speaking honestly with God, even when words feel hard to find.

- A Reflection Question to help you pause and make the truth personal, inviting joy to take root in your own story.

My hope is that you will not rush through these pages, but instead, take time with each day. Allow the Word to settle deeply in your heart. Let the prayer shape your conversation with God. And let the reflection question challenge you to grow.

This is more than a book—it's an invitation to rediscover joy, one day at a time.

With love and encouragement,

Ruthie

The Joy Scriptures

1. Philippians 4:4
2. Nehemiah 8:10
3. Psalm 16:11
4. Romans 15:13
5. Psalm 28:7
6. Psalm 21:6
7. Psalm 92:4
8. 1 Thessalonians 5:16–18
9. James 1:2–3
10. Psalm 51:12
11. Psalm 19:8
12. Jeremiah 15:16
13. Psalm 95:1
14. Psalm 5:11
15. Psalm 97:1–2
16. Lamentations 3:22–23
17. Psalm 19:1
18. Job 8:21
19. 1 Peter 1:8
20. Isaiah 26:3
21. Revelation 21:4
22. Isaiah 12:3
23. Psalm 81:1

24. Isaiah 35:10b
25. 2 Corinthians 8:4
26. John 15:11
27. Psalm 118:14
28. Philippians 2:2
29. Philippians 4:4
30. John 16:24

THE ENCOURAGEMENT SERIES
ONE-MONTH DEVOTIONAL

"REJOICE IN THE LORD ALWAYS;
AGAIN I WILL SAY, REJOICE." —PHILIPPIANS 4:4

JOY IN HIS PRESENCE

Joy in the Lord is not dependent on circumstances; it is a choice to focus on His goodness. Paul wrote these words while imprisoned, proving that true joy transcends life's hardships. When we set our hearts on Christ, we find a wellspring of joy that no trial can steal.

Lord, help me to find joy in You today. No matter what comes my way, let my heart be anchored in the truth of Your love. Fill me with a deep, abiding joy that is not shaken by life's ups and downs. I choose to rejoice in You. Amen.

Reflective Question:

When was the last time you felt overwhelming joy in God's presence?

"DO NOT GRIEVE, FOR THE JOY OF THE LORD IS YOUR STRENGTH." —NEHEMIAH 8:10

When life feels overwhelming, God's joy sustains us. This joy is not fleeting happiness but a deep, abiding strength that fuels perseverance. Lean into His presence, and let His joy be your refuge and power in every situation.

Lord, help me to find my strength in Your joy. Remind me that no matter my circumstances, Your joy is my anchor. Amen.

Reflective Question:

In what situation today do you most need to lean on God's joy for strength?

"YOU MAKE KNOWN TO ME THE PATH OF LIFE; IN YOUR PRESENCE THERE IS FULLNESS OF JOY; AT YOUR RIGHT HAND ARE PLEASURES FOREVERMORE."
—PSALM 16:11

JOY IN GOD'S PRESENCE

True joy is found in God's presence, not in temporary pleasures. When we walk with Him, He reveals a life rich in purpose, peace, and delight. Seek Him daily, and experience the fullness of joy that only He can give.

Lord, help me to look to You and seek Your presence daily and find my joy in You alone. Amen.

Reflective Question:

What worries and distractions do you need to set aside to experience fullness of joy in God's presence?

"MAY THE GOD OF HOPE FILL YOU WITH ALL JOY AND PEACE IN BELIEVING, SO THAT BY THE POWER OF THE HOLY SPIRIT YOU MAY ABOUND IN HOPE." —ROMANS 15:13

JOY IN GOD'S SALVATION

Faith in God brings a joy that is deeply rooted in hope. The Holy Spirit fills our hearts with peace, even in uncertain times, reminding us that our future is secure in Him. Trust in His promises, and let joy overflow in your life.

Dear God, thank You for being my source of joy and peace. Help me to trust in You more each day and to find joy in the journey, knowing that You are with me every step of the way. Amen.

Reflective Question:

How can you trust God more in your current journey and allow His joy and peace to fill your heart?

"THE LORD IS MY STRENGTH AND MY SHIELD; MY HEART TRUSTS IN HIM, AND HE HELPS ME. MY HEART LEAPS FOR JOY, AND WITH MY SONG I PRAISE HIM." —PSALM 28:7

JOY THROUGH TRUST

Trust is the doorway to joy. When we place our confidence in God's care, our hearts are free from fear, and joy naturally follows. Knowing that He is both our protector and provider gives us a reason to sing —even before the breakthrough comes.

Lord, increase my trust in You so my heart may leap for joy in all circumstances. Amen.

Reflective Question:

Where in your life can you replace worry with trust today?

"SURELY YOU HAVE GRANTED HIM
UNENDING BLESSINGS AND MADE HIM
GLAD WITH THE JOY OF YOUR PRESENCE."
—PSALM 21:6

JOY IN GOD'S PRESENCE ALWAYS

The greatest blessing God gives is Himself. His presence is not just a comfort—it's a source of continual joy. We may lose many things in this life, but we will never lose His nearness. That promise is a gift that outlasts every season.

Lord, thank You for the unending joy of Your presence. Help me to live every day aware that You are with me. Amen.

Reflective Question:

How can you make time in your schedule to sit in God's presence today and experience His joy?

"FOR YOU MAKE ME GLAD BY YOUR DEEDS, LORD; I SING FOR JOY AT WHAT YOUR HANDS HAVE DONE."
—PSALM 92:4

JOY FROM REMEMBERING HIS WORKS

When we stop to remember what God has done—both in the Bible and in our own lives—joy rises in our hearts. Gratitude feeds joy, and worship is the natural response. His past faithfulness reminds us that He will continue to act on our behalf.

Lord, remind me daily of Your good works so my heart may overflow with joy and gratitude. Amen.

Reflective Question:
What is one specific thing God has done for you that still makes your heart sing?

"REJOICE ALWAYS."
—1 THESSALONIANS 5:16

REJOICING ALWAYS

Joy, prayer, and gratitude are not just occasional acts but a lifestyle. Even in hardship, we can remain joyful by staying connected to God in prayer and finding reasons to give thanks. This is how we walk in God's will daily.

Lord, teach me to rejoice in every season, trusting in Your perfect plan. Amen.

Reflective Question:
What is one small thing you can give thanks for today?

"CONSIDER IT PURE JOY, MY BROTHERS AND SISTERS, WHENEVER YOU FACE TRIALS OF MANY KINDS." —JAMES 1:2

JOY IN TRIALS

Joy in trials doesn't come naturally —it comes supernaturally. God uses hardship to grow our faith and produce spiritual endurance. When we see trials through His perspective, we can rejoice, knowing they are shaping us to be more like Christ.

Lord, help me to see my trials as opportunities for growth, and let joy be my response. Amen.

Reflective Question:

What would it look like to choose joy in the trial you are walking through today?

"RESTORE TO ME THE JOY OF YOUR SALVATION AND GRANT ME A WILLING SPIRIT, TO SUSTAIN ME." —PSALM 51:12

JOY IN GOD'S SALVATION

True joy begins with salvation. When we remember what God has done for us, our hearts overflow with gratitude and gladness.

Father, renew my heart with the joy of Your salvation. Keep my spirit willing to follow You each day. Amen.

Reflective Question:
How can you remind yourself daily of the joy of your salvation?

DAY 10

"THE PRECEPTS OF THE LORD ARE RIGHT, GIVING JOY TO THE HEART." —PSALM 19:8

JOY IN OBEDIENCE

God's commands are not burdens —they are pathways to joy. When we walk in His ways, we experience peace, purpose, and the deep satisfaction of living in alignment with His will. Obedience brings freedom, and freedom brings joy.

Lord, help me to delight in Your commands and obey You with a joyful heart. Amen.

Reflective Question:

What is one step of obedience you can take today that will lead to joy?

"WHEN YOUR WORDS CAME, I ATE THEM; THEY WERE MY JOY AND MY HEART'S DELIGHT."
—JEREMIAH 15:16

JOY IN GOD'S WORD

God's Word brings joy to those who receive it. When we take in His truth and let it dwell in our hearts, it becomes a source of delight. His Word reminds us that we are called and cherished by Him.

Father, let Your Word be the joy of my heart. Teach me to treasure Your truth and to find delight in being called by Your name. Amen.

Reflective Question:
In what ways has Scripture encouraged your heart this week?

"COME, LET US SING FOR JOY TO THE LORD;
LET US SHOUT ALOUD TO THE ROCK OF
OUR SALVATION." —PSALM 95:1

JOY IN WORSHIP

Worship is an overflow of joy, and joy grows stronger when we worship. When we sing, pray, and praise, we lift our eyes above life's struggles and fix them on God's greatness. Joy is both the reason for worship and the result of it.

Lord, fill my heart with songs of joy as I worship You today. Amen.

Reflective Question:

What song of praise can you sing today to express your gratitude?

"BUT LET ALL WHO TAKE REFUGE IN YOU BE GLAD; LET THEM EVER SING FOR JOY. SPREAD YOUR PROTECTION OVER THEM, THAT THOSE WHO LOVE YOUR NAME MAY REJOICE IN YOU." —PSALM 5:11

JOY IN GOD'S PROTECTION

Joy is found in the security of God's protection. When we take refuge in Him, we can rejoice without fear, knowing that He is our defender and our safe place.

Thank You, Lord, for being my refuge. I rejoice in the safety of Your care. Amen.

Reflective Question:

How does knowing God protects you change the way you approach challenges?

"THE LORD REIGNS, LET THE EARTH BE GLAD; LET THE DISTANT SHORES REJOICE. CLOUDS AND THICK DARKNESS SURROUND HIM; RIGHTEOUSNESS AND JUSTICE ARE THE FOUNDATION OF HIS THRONE."
—PSALM 97:1–2

We can rejoice because God is perfectly just. In a world of injustice, He is the righteous Judge who will set all things right. His justice is not harsh—it flows from His love and ensures that His kingdom is one of peace and joy.

Lord, I rejoice that You reign with justice and righteousness. Help me to trust in Your perfect judgment. Amen.

Reflective Question:
Where do you need to trust God's justice instead of seeking your own?

"BECAUSE OF THE LORD'S GREAT LOVE WE ARE NOT CONSUMED, FOR HIS COMPASSIONS NEVER FAIL. THEY ARE NEW EVERY MORNING; GREAT IS YOUR FAITHFULNESS." —LAMENTATIONS 3:22-23

GOD'S STEADFAST LOVE

Each morning brings a fresh wave of God's mercy and compassion. His love is unshakable, carrying us through every hardship. No failure or trial can exhaust His kindness toward us.

Lord, thank You for Your unfailing love and new mercies each day. Amen.

Reflective Question:
How has God shown you His compassion in a difficult season?

DAY 16

"THE HEAVENS DECLARE THE GLORY OF GOD; THE SKIES PROCLAIM THE WORK OF HIS HANDS." —PSALM 19:1

JOY IN GOD'S CREATION

The beauty of creation serves as a reminder of God's greatness and care. Taking time to notice His handiwork can fill our hearts with gratitude and joy.

Lord, open my eyes to see Your glory in all You have made. Amen.

Reflective Question:
Where in nature do you most feel God's joy?

"HE WILL YET FILL YOUR MOUTH WITH LAUGHTER AND YOUR LIPS WITH SHOUTS OF JOY." —JOB 8:21

THE GIFT OF LAUGHTER

God delights in seeing His children rejoice. Even in seasons of loss, He promises to restore our laughter. Joy doesn't always come in the form of big victories—sometimes it's the quiet moments of relief, gratitude, or a shared smile that remind us He is present and working for our good.

Father, thank You for the gift of joy and laughter. Restore my spirit so that I may rejoice in You again. Amen.

DAY 18

Reflective Question:
How has God restored joy or laughter in your life after a time of sorrow?

"THOUGH YOU HAVE NOT SEEN HIM, YOU LOVE HIM; AND EVEN THOUGH YOU DO NOT SEE HIM NOW, YOU BELIEVE IN HIM AND ARE FILLED WITH AN INEXPRESSIBLE AND GLORIOUS JOY." —1 PETER 1:8

UNSHAKEABLE JOY

Faith brings an inexpressible joy—one that is not based on what we see but on the hope of eternity. Even though we have not physically seen Jesus, our hearts are filled with His presence, and that fills us with glorious joy.

Jesus, I believe in You and rejoice in the salvation You have given me. Fill my heart with inexpressible joy as I walk in faith and trust Your promises. Amen.

Reflective Question:
How does your faith in Christ bring you joy in ways the world cannot?

"YOU WILL KEEP IN PERFECT PEACE THOSE WHOSE MINDS ARE STEADFAST, BECAUSE THEY TRUST IN YOU." —ISAIAH 26:3

GOD'S PERFECT PEACE

Perfect peace comes from fixing our thoughts on God and trusting Him fully. When our focus is on His unchanging character rather than our shifting circumstances, our hearts remain calm and steady.

Lord, help me keep my mind fixed on You. Amen.

Reflective Question:

What helps you keep your mind anchored in God's truth?

"HE WILL WIPE AWAY EVERY TEAR FROM THEIR EYES, AND DEATH SHALL BE NO MORE, NEITHER SHALL THERE BE MOURNING, NOR CRYING, NOR PAIN ANYMORE, FOR THE FORMER THINGS HAVE PASSED AWAY."
—REVELATION 21:4

JOY FROM GOD'S FAITHFULNESS

The promise of eternal joy is a source of immense hope and comfort. Revelation 21:4 paints a beautiful picture of the future where there will be no more tears, death, mourning, or pain. This eternal joy is our ultimate hope as believers.

Heavenly Father, thank you for the promise of eternal joy. Help me to hold onto this hope and to find joy in the assurance of Your future kingdom. Amen.

Reflective Question:
What "great thing" has God done for you recently?

"WITH JOY YOU WILL DRAW WATER FROM THE WELLS OF SALVATION." —ISAIAH 12:3

JOY IN SALVATION

Our salvation is the greatest source of joy, a well that never runs dry. No matter what is happening in life, the fact that we are saved and secure in Christ is reason enough to rejoice daily.

Thank You, Lord, for the gift of salvation. May I never take it for granted, but draw joy from it daily. Amen.

Reflective Question:

How often do you take time to thank God for the joy of your salvation?

"SING FOR JOY TO GOD OUR STRENGTH;
SHOUT ALOUD TO THE GOD OF JACOB!"
—PSALM 81:1

SINGING FOR JOY

Praise fuels joy. When we sing to God—whether through music or simply with words of gratitude—we shift our focus from problems to His greatness, and joy rises within us.

Father, help me to lift my voice in praise, no matter my circumstances. Amen.

Reflective Question:
How does worship impact your level of joy?

"GLADNESS AND JOY WILL OVERTAKE THEM, AND SORROW AND SIGHING WILL FLEE AWAY." —ISAIAH 35:10B

EVERLASTING JOY

In Christ, our future is secure. One day, sorrow will vanish completely, and joy will overtake us forever. By keeping our eyes on God's eternal promise, we can face life's passing troubles with hope and joyful expectation.

Lord, help me to keep my eyes fixed on the joy that awaits in eternity with You. Amen.

Reflective Question:

How does remembering eternity change your perspective on today's struggles?

"THEY URGENTLY PLEADED WITH US FOR THE PRIVILEGE OF SHARING IN THIS SERVICE TO THE LORD'S PEOPLE."
—2 CORINTHIANS 8:4

JOY THROUGH GENEROSITY

There is joy in giving—especially when it's done willingly and out of love. Generosity connects us to God's heart and brings us joy as we bless others.

Lord, help me give with a cheerful heart and find joy in serving others. Amen.

Reflective Question:
When was the last time giving brought you unexpected joy?

"THESE THINGS I HAVE SPOKEN TO YOU, THAT MY JOY MAY BE IN YOU, AND THAT YOUR JOY MAY BE FULL." —JOHN 15:11

A HEART FULL OF JOY

Jesus offers us His own joy—a joy that is complete and not dependent on circumstances. It's a gift meant to fill our hearts, empowering us to live abundantly.

Lord Jesus, thank You for the fullness of joy that comes from abiding in You. Help me to let go of temporary satisfactions and seek Your lasting joy every day. Amen.

Reflective Question:

Is there something fleeting you're holding onto instead of lasting joy? How can you turn your heart toward the deeper joy found in Christ?

"THE LORD IS MY STRENGTH AND MY DEFENSE; HE HAS BECOME MY SALVATION."
—PSALM 118:14

THE JOY OF THE LORD IS MY SONG

Our joy is expressed not only in smiles and words but also in the songs of our hearts. God's salvation gives us reason to sing, even in life's storms.

Lord, let my life be a song of joy and gratitude to You. Amen.

Reflective Question:
If your life were a song of joy, what would its main theme be?

"MAKE MY JOY COMPLETE BY BEING LIKE-MINDED, HAVING THE SAME LOVE, BEING ONE IN SPIRIT AND OF ONE MIND."
—PHILIPPIANS 2:2

SHARING JOY WITH OTHERS

Unity and love among believers deepen our joy. When we live in harmony, we reflect Christ's love to the world.

Lord, help me to pursue unity and share Your joy with those around me. Amen.

Reflective Question:
How can you bring joy to someone else today?

"IT IS MORE BLESSED TO GIVE THAN TO RECEIVE." —ACTS 20:35

JOY IN SERVING

Serving others brings joy because it reflects the heart of Christ. By giving of ourselves, we experience the blessing of being His hands and feet.

Lord, help me to serve with joy, knowing I am serving You. Amen.

Reflective Question:
What act of service can you do this week to bring joy to others?

DAY 29

"ASK AND YOU WILL RECEIVE, AND YOUR JOY WILL BE COMPLETE." —JOHN 16:24

JOY IN ANSWERED PRAYER

Jesus invites us to bring our needs to Him. As we trust and ask in His name, He answers in ways that fill us with joy. This joy comes from knowing that God hears us and is faithful to provide what we need.

Jesus, thank You for the invitation to bring my needs to You. Teach me to trust in Your name and to find fullness of joy in Your answers. Amen.

DAY 30

Reflective Question:
How has God answered a prayer in a way that brought you joy?

A Final Thought

As you close this book, remember—real joy doesn't come from circumstances but from the presence of God. My prayer is that the verses, reflections, and prayers you've read have planted seeds of hope in your heart and reminded you of His unchanging faithfulness.

Carry these words with you, return to them when you need encouragement, and share them with others who long for joy. This is just the beginning of the journey. May you continue to grow in faith, walk in God's strength, and live each day with His joy overflowing in your life.

About the Author

Ruth Hovsepian is an international speaker, author, and podcast host passionate about encouraging people to live with faith, courage, and hope. With honesty and vulnerability, she shares her journey of brokenness and redemption, reminding others that God's grace meets us right where we are.

Through her books, devotionals, and speaking, Ruth combines Scripture with personal experience to offer practical wisdom and encouragement. Her simple yet powerful style makes the truths of the Bible accessible to both lifelong believers and those still searching.

When she isn't writing or speaking, Ruth enjoys time with her family, mentoring women, and serving in her church. Her latest project, The Encouragement Series, was created to provide daily inspiration and hope through Scripture, prayer, and reflection.

More From Ruth

100 DAYS OF PRAYER

Prayer changes everything—but sometimes, finding the words can be hard. *100 Days of Prayer* provides simple, heartfelt prayers rooted in Scripture to guide you day by day. Each prayer is designed to draw you closer to God, strengthen your faith, and give you words to speak in every season of life. Whether you're overwhelmed, grateful, or in need of encouragement, this book will be your companion in building a deeper, more consistent prayer life. Perfect for personal devotion, small groups, or as a gift for someone you love.

Prepare Him Room

This Christmas devotional invites you to slow down and create space in your heart for Christ. Filled with short daily reflections, Scripture, and simple prayers, *Prepare Him Room* leads you through the wonder of Advent—expectation, waiting, and quiet rejoicing. Each entry offers a practical way to mark the season with meaning: a moment of stillness, a family reading, or a heartfelt prayer. Warm, tender, and beautifully paced, this book is an ideal gift for those who want a more reflective, faith-centered holiday.

THE ULTIMATE CONVERSATION:
IS THAT YOU, GOD?

Are you listening for God's voice but unsure how to tell it apart from your own thoughts? *The Ultimate Conversation* is a practical, soul-stirring Bible study that helps you recognize God's presence and respond with faith. Through Scripture readings, clear teaching, and guided questions, Ruth walks you step-by-step into habits of discernment—listening prayer, quiet reflection, and biblical testing of impressions. Perfect for small groups or personal study, this book equips you to move from spiritual confusion to confident conversation with God. If you long for clearer direction and a deeper relationship with the Lord, this study will change the way you hear and follow Him.

A MOTHER'S LOVE:
A HEARTFELT JOURNEY

An illustrated collection of poetic reflections, *A Mother's Love* celebrates the tender, messy, sacred work of motherhood. With lyrical verse and evocative artwork on every page, this keepsake honors the everyday moments—sleepless nights, first steps, quiet prayers—while pointing to the deep heart of love that shapes a family. Short enough to read in a single sitting, yet rich enough to return to again and again, this book makes a meaningful gift for new moms, grandmothers, or anyone who cherishes the beauty of maternal love.